Made in United States
Troutdale, OR
11/23/2023

14481972R10070